Thank you for
your continued
support!
Deane

What others are saying about Deana Carter and this book

"After being happily married (I thought) for 30 years, raising triplets and watching them succeed, the man I trusted devastated me in a single, long-distance phone call (he was on the other side of the country; I was in Walmart). My friend Deana helped me navigate this unnerving transition emotionally and with sage financial advice. Deana's book is amazing, info-packed, humorous and fun to read. I LOVE it and know you will too. I plan to buy dozens of copies to give friends and family so they will be prepared, not naively blindsided as I was!" ~ Jill Stiker

"After reading this book, I recommend it to anyone contemplating or undergoing a separation, divorce or widowhood. Better to have this info before the fact. I had never heard of a CDFA, but Deana is one, and she is an invaluable asset in this arena." ~ Ellen Greenhill

"Deana's book provides insight into complicated issues in easy to understand language and her breezy writing style keeps the reader's attention. Her exhortation to "Be Prepared" should be heeded by all. Her animated writing helps readers learn about topics like how Social Security and domestic relations orders effect divorce proceedings without being overwhelmed. I recommend this book to all married women to become prepared and empowered. Knowledge is empowerment." ~ Beatrice Snider, Law Office of Beatrice Snider, APC

"For twenty years, my financial philosophy was to make sure my wife had enough when I died. But God laughs when you tell her your plans. Deana has written an important book for surviving spouses. I recommend considering all options and I highly recommend her book." ~ Richard P. Edwards, Esq

"With more than 26 years of financial planning experience from estate planning to divorce Deana has written a book that provides a wealth of useful information for women of all ages faced with a critical, life altering change." ~ Vincent Bartolotta, Senior Managing Partner, Thorsnes Bartolotta Mcguire LLP

"I commend Deana for sharing her considerable knowledge in this groundbreaking book, which can save women from financial and emotional devastation during a critical time. Thanks to the wit and wisdom contained herein, thousands of newly divorced female readers will be laughing… all the way to the bank!" ~ Roxana Foxx, Founder/CEO, Hunter International

"Chock-full of priceless information, this powerful and dynamite book empowers, encourages and guides women to take charge of their finances and prosper after death or divorce." ~ Susan Friedmann, CSP, international bestselling author of *Riches in Niches: How to Make it BIG in a small Market*

"Even though this is *"A Woman's Guide to Maintaining Financial Wealth and Well-Being Upon Divorce or Spousal Death,"* I recommend it to anyone. Deana outlines the basics and in-depth details about investing, the importance of good credit, financial planning, life insurance and much more. Better yet, this book should be required reading before you marry. Knowing the facts presented in this book gives one the tools to make informed decisions that are wise in the short- and long-term." ~ Annie M. Fonte, MBA, Author, *Keep Your Ass In The Saddle*

"Provides practical advice in plain language at a time when your world is spinning. The information can help the reader get a plan together to help stabilize their world. Two thumbs up!" ~ Jeffrey C. Siegel, Ph.D., ABPP

"This book is a refreshing look at everything you need to know before your spouse dies or you kick him to the curb. Deana Carter walks you through everything from life insurance to collecting your share of your spouse's Social Security and getting back into the dating game. This is the kind of book every woman--and maybe some husbands if they're smart--will want to read and keep in their purses for quick, easy, and frequent reference." ~ Tyler R. Tichelaar, PhD and award-winning author of *Narrow Lives* and *The Best Place*

WHAT TO DO IF YOU BOOT HIM OR BURY HIM

A Woman's Guide to Maintaining Financial Wealth and Well-Being Upon Divorce or Spousal Death

Deana Carter
CLU, ChFC, CDFA

AVIVA
PUBLISHING
New York

Published by:
Aviva Publishing
Lake Placid, NY
518-523-1320
www.avivapubs.com

ISBN: 978-1-950241-68-2
Library of Congress Control Number: TXu 2-173-674

Editor: Tyler Tichelaar, Superior Book Productions
Layout: Larry Alexander, Superior Book Productions

Dedication

This book is dedicated to the numerous female clients
I have been able to guide through the challenging and
frequently raging waters of divorce,
and to every woman who reads, absorbs,
and uses the information contained within these pages.
You are all my heroes.

Contents

Foreword

WHEN I BEGAN MY CAREER as an entrepreneur, I had already learned the importance of money, savings, and limiting spending habits because of earning an income as a child, doing door-to-door sales, having a paper route, and shoveling snow. However, I did not realize the power of these lessons instilled in me at a young age.

As I got older, I watched more and more people spend money without restraint and accumulate all this "stuff." So many of us have fallen into the trap that teaches us materialism and stuff make us happy. Some call shopping a form of "therapy." I am not sure if that is true, but I am certainly guilty of it at times.

I began to ask: Why are some people very wealthy and some people very poor? And what I found out was that the wealthiest people I know live as if they are poor and spend very little on things they may or may not need. Poor people often get over their heads in debt because they live as though they are wealthy and spend more than they earn.

This habit over a long period of time leads to a recipe for disaster.

I discovered that people who were born poor (in many cases) actually die rich because they have learned the importance of money at a young age and develop a solid work ethic. Conversely (not always but in many cases), people who were born rich, die poor because they never develop a work ethic and have a sense of entitlement. Sometimes this attitude works for them, but often it does not.

Successful people have learned to take 100% responsibility for their lives. They let go, forgive, move on, and take the lessons from all their adversities to make a better life for themselves, financially and otherwise.

In this powerful book by Deana Carter, owner/operator of Carter Financial, directed primarily toward women, you will learn how to prepare for divorce before the subject is broached and also how to plan for spousal death. And even though the title of this book is a bit humorous, Deana teaches rock solid financial principles that will serve the test of time for both women and men. Even though there is a lot of humor in this book, don't let that mislead you about the power, wisdom, and expertise Deana shares to help you preserve and protect your assets.

Divorce can be devastating emotionally and financially. In *What to Do If You Boot Him or Bury Him*, Deana provides you with the fundamentals of finance that every woman should know before she races to the divorce attorney. If you follow the experience and techniques offered in this book, not only can you save thousands of dollars, but potentially years of time. You will benefit from her successful track record as a skilled and insightful financial advisor to keep you, your money, and your financial future intact.

When you learn why to remove your emotions from negotiations, and follow strategies such as how to get your fair share of your soon-to-be-ex's retirement and how to invest wisely and well, you will discover how you can move forward, protecting your lifestyle and how to be confidently poised for your future.

You will learn how to acquire specific knowledge about everything from Social Security and Medicare to life insurance, retaining the marital home or choosing to downsize, and much more.

Through this book, you will learn that you are the driver of your better tomorrow. You are the captain of your ship; you are the creator of your destiny. Most importantly, you will learn how to be the "victor" of your life and finances instead of being the "victim."

Let Deana Carter be the driving force to assist you on your journey. Best wishes and get ready for an amazing ride! And by the way, I am hopeful that I will not be "booted" or "buried," and I suspect, whether you are male or female, you feel the same way. That was supposed to be a bit of humor, letting you know it's okay to smile and laugh as you dive into this book.

Patrick Snow

Publishing Coach, Professional Speaker,
and International Best-Selling Author of
Creating Your Own Destiny,
The Affluent Entrepreneur,
and *Boy Entrepreneur*

www.PatrickSnow.com
www.ThePublishingDoctor.com

Introduction

"And so, Cinderella and the Prince were
married, and they lived happily ever after."

— Grimms' Fairy Tales

BLAME NINETEENTH CENTURY GERMAN FAIRY tales for the romantic marriage fantasy many young women have grown up quixotically hoping to achieve. Brothers Grimm classics such as "Snow White and the Seven Dwarfs" and "Cinderella" contain harrowing, even gruesome, moments, but not to worry: the stories magically culminate in a wedding between the beautiful bride and her dashing prince, whereupon the ecstatically happy husband and wife depart to their splendid castle (without evil stepmothers but with devoted servants) to live happily ever after.

The reality is far less Grimm and far more grim. According to the 2010 U.S. Census, America has the tenth highest divorce rate in the world: 53%. That equates to one divorce every six seconds. Since many divorces occur later in life, it's no surprise that, as the National Institute on Retirement Security reports, 80% of women are likely to fall into poverty in their retirement years.

If the husband you supported emotionally, sexually, and perhaps even financially while he pursued a professional degree does not leave you for the yoga instructor who was in diapers when you were attending your high school prom, chances are he will die before you.

Eight out of ten women outlive their husbands. Nearly half of widows say they wished they'd taken a more active role in their finances prior to their husband's death.

Goodbye, Marriage; Hello, Retirement Insecurity!

In high-stress circumstances such as divorce or death, you may be too startled, frightened, or disarrayed to think and act judiciously on your own behalf. In the first instance, you might have no clue what is going on until hubby says (or calls or emails or texts) four words: "I want a divorce." In the second case, you may be devoting your entire being to nursing him lovingly through a worsening chronic disease and not have the time or energy to think about yourself, until suddenly the worst has happened, the funeral is over, your house is empty, and you realize you don't have a credit card in your own name.

As you can see, the end of the fairy tale will at some point be followed by the beginning of a new stage of your life. You want to make sure you are the driver of that stage, not the one being driven into financial insecurity.

I wrote this book to prepare and empower you to take control of your finances and your future; to provide you with the knowledge and confidence to choose a financial plan that meets your needs today, tomorrow, and twenty years from now. It will educate you about government programs such as Social Security and Medicare, help you navigate investment options, and guide you to finding a trusted financial advisor who will partner with you on your quest.

Ready to begin? Take a deep breath, turn the page, and let's get started!

IT'S A FACT

The U.S. rate of divorce after age fifty has doubled since 1990. These "gray divorces" take a major toll on the financial health of both husband and wife, but they are particularly devastating for women.

Source: Bowling Green State University, National Center for Family & Marriage Research

Chapter 1

'Til Divorce Do Us Part ... Prepare Before You Share the News

"I'm not upset about my divorce. I'm only upset I'm not a widow."

— *Roseanne Barr*

THE BEST TIME TO PLAN for divorce is light years before the subject comes up, but frequently, this life-altering ordeal is suddenly thrust upon you. With meticulous preparation, you could have protected yourself and the nest egg you've wisely been stashing away. But you still can.

Don't think divorce could happen to you? We all know that lovey-dovey, ostensibly happily-married couple who, to everyone's surprise, after twenty or even thirty years of marriage, suddenly announces they are splitting up.

Divorce, especially later in life, can be emotionally and financially devastating for both parties. As noted by Dr. Susan Brown, co-author of *The Gray Divorce Revolution*, while post-divorce household income drops approximately 25% for men, it plummets more than 40% for women. This depressing scenario is exacerbated for women who have been out of the work force for years, making their current financial status and their future retirement security, lifestyle, and health much more precarious.

IT'S A FACT

In 2014, nearly one million divorces took place in the United States.

Source: Centers for Disease Control and Prevention (CDC), National Center for Health Statistics

You Need a Well-Thought-Out Divorce Plan

If rain is in the forecast, you grab your umbrella when you head out the door, so why would you not want to be equally prepared for what could be the largest financial transaction of your life?

Making prudent decisions, with the assistance of a financial advisor/advocate to protect your personal finances, is most effectively done before divorce or death leaves you suddenly single. Hasty, emotionally-driven decisions could have lasting deleterious effects. Do not wait for a storm of critical decisions that need to be made immediately when you can instead have your umbrella of safety measures ready through advanced planning about how to divide assets, budget on a single income, calculate future retirement and healthcare needs, and more.

We will delve into the following and other topics in depth in later chapters, but here is a brief overview of some important preparations you can and should make now. Let me repeat: NOW!

As Alexander Graham Bell wisely said, "Before anything else, preparation is the key to success."

1. Find a competent Certified Divorce Financial Advisor (CDFA). Make sure your advisor is someone you feel comfortable with and can rely on to provide comprehensive information and candid advice. This financial partner can coordinate the process with other professionals and will always have your back.

2. Collect, store, and update your records. Make print or digital (or both) copies of tax returns, loan documents, wills/trusts, banking and brokerage statements, credit card statements, deeds to property, car registrations, insurance policies, and other documents. Pay special attention to any records that verify property solely in your name—such as an inheritance. You will need to update many of these documents after a divorce or death.

IT'S A FACT

Exercise extreme caution when dividing assets and shifting ownership. You will want to review options for alimony, paying heed to tax consequences. To avoid substantial tax burdens, check with your CDFA or tax advisor before signing anything.

3. Go on a treasure hunt. In this case, you are looking not only for assets your divorcing spouse has squirreled away unbeknownst to you, but even more frightening, hidden debt. In community property states such as California, you generally will be held responsible for half of your spouse's debt—even if the debt is only in his name. Not fair, you say? You're correct; yet life is not always fair. But (to cite a cliché) knowledge is power.

IT'S A FACT

Did you help put your spouse through medical, dental, or law school? You may be eligible for a portion of tuition reimbursement.

4. Document belongings. Make a photo file of your jewelry, art, and other valuables—whether the value is monetary or sentimental.

5. Review your credit scores. (Annualcreditreport. com offers free yearly credit reports.) If you do not have a credit card in your name alone, this would be an excellent time to obtain one. Need you tell him? No!

6. Prepare for the results of asset division and other financial realities. You can prepare for financial changes by learning about rolling over retirement assets, checking Social Security benefits, and evaluating your insurance needs (life, health, disability, long-term care). Plan to adjust your income and budget, including discretionary spending.

7. Don't do the obvious thing. Do the smart thing. We women tend to be nesters. When faced with losing your marriage (even if you initiate the split), the last thing you may feel you can bear to lose is your house. Planning ahead can help you avoid an emotionally fraught decision. Keeping the house may be a burden, not a boon. It may not be a good financial choice for you, in terms of property taxes, ongoing maintenance, and unexpected expenses. (And remember: He might not have been a great husband, but hubby was handy at fixing things you now will have to pay to have repaired.) In today's volatile economic times, you cannot count on the value of your home increasing steadily should you choose to sell it down the road. You may bravely want to make a fresh start now.

IT'S A FACT

According to California law, if a marriage has lasted longer than ten years, the spouse with less money may ask for financial support. If you have the most, a gray divorce could put you in the red for spousal support.

Return to Number 1

I know this To-Do List appears daunting. If you are contemplating—or in the midst of—a (possibly messy) divorce, the process can be overwhelming. That is why Number 1 is so vital.

You would not attempt to perform major surgery on yourself. Similarly, you need a CDFA professional to help you get through this major surgery of marriage dissolution so you can recover quickly and remain happy, prosperous, and whole.

Avoid Perils and Pitfalls

An impending divorce is frequently traumatizing. It can also be financially debilitating, so it is important to "know before you go" visit a professional. Many accountants, financial planners, and attorneys, although skilled in their chosen fields, do not have the necessary, intricate knowledge of divorce financials and may not realize they do not possess this knowledge. Mistakes made during the dissolution process have long-term consequences.

Common mistakes made by professionals with limited divorce finance experience include:

- May not obtain or properly evaluate retirement plans, pension plans, employee benefits, stock options, assets, debts, and other settlement-related issues.
- May not understand the purpose and optimum timing of a Qualified Domestic Relations Order (QDRO).
- May not protect or structure spousal and child support payments, survivor benefits, and the like.

Benefits of Partnering with a CDFA

Only 5,000 financial advisors in the U.S. have successfully completed the challenging curriculum to become a Certified Divorce Financial Analyst (CDFA) through the

Institute for Divorce Financial Analysts (IDFA). The IDFA, to quote its website, is "the premier national organization dedicated to the certification, education, and promotion of the use of financial professionals in the divorce arena."

I attained this pinnacle of certification so I could help people—primarily women—prepare for and address the challenges of divorce.

CDFAs coordinate the process and provide you with the total package, including litigation support. We complete the detailed financial work that makes case preparation and settlements go more smoothly and successfully in your favor. We can refer you to an appropriate attorney, forensic accountant, and other professionals, wrapping you in a warm circle of support.

While helping determine your short- and long-term financial goals during this arduous time, a CDFA can perform a detail-rich lifestyle analysis preceding spousal support claims. The analysis painstakingly examines marital spending to calculate the amount of money you will require to maintain your pre-divorce lifestyle. It also can detect a husband's "hidden" expenditures, such as affairs and fraudulent third-party conveyances.

An Asset Crowd in the Cloud

From Beatles albums to books to Bitcoin—not to mention airline miles and hotel points—digital assets are now a force to be reckoned with, and they are frequently fought over during divorce negotiations.

A digital asset is an item that can be stored digitally, has value, and cannot be easily or inexpensively reproduced. Today, many couples' digital assets exceed $50,000, including photos, movies, games, and the accounts used to purchase such items.

When accounts are in both names, the division of property becomes more problematic. And if one spouse wants to stick it to the other, they can refuse to give it to you. In some cases, the transfer may be impossible. If you've downloaded tons of books on your husband's Kindle, and he is the sole owner of that account, his signed user agreement may restrict him from giving you the rights to it.

As your CDFA advocate, I can recommend a viable approach to the division of digital assets, including those of significant monetary value and items like family photos that are of significant sentimental value. As with all assets, the goal is to help clients find an equitable division.

Chapter 2

Social Security

*"I was too old for a paper route, too young for
Social Security, and too tired for an affair."*
— *Erma Bombeck*

WHEN WORKING TOWARD A DIVORCE settlement,
Social Security benefits, unlike assets such as real
estate and personal investments, are not negotiable. But
it is vitally important to your financial wellbeing as you
age to understand this government program. You will
need to know minutiae such as the difference between
divorced spousal benefits and divorced survivor benefits,
and you should strategize in advance on how to maximize
your benefits over your lifetime.

Social Security has provided financial protection to
Americans since 1935. Offering retirement, disability,
and survivor benefits, Social Security is one of the most
successful anti-poverty programs in our nation's history.
However, it is a complex, multifaceted program that can

be bewildering. You must become educated so you can make informed decisions about your retirement.

One thing to remember: Social Security is intended to supplement one's retirement income, not provide the sole source of income. Unfortunately, many people living in or close to poverty are forced to rely totally on this government program.

IT'S A FACT

By 2050, almost 90% of divorced Social Security spousal beneficiaries aged 62 or older will be women. They will receive all or part of their benefits based on their ex-spouse's earnings.

Source: Bowling Green State University, National Center for Family & Marriage Research

Unpacking Rules, Restrictions, and Benefits

The two-word tagline for any government program from Social Security, Medicare, and the IRS to a dreaded DMV appointment could be: "It's complicated."

The jargon can be intimidating, and the conglomeration of numbers and percentages can be difficult to parse, for example: "If full retirement age is 65, a spouse can get 37.5 percent of the worker's unreduced benefit at age 62." For that reason, I will present some relevant information regarding Social Security benefits paid to a spouse upon divorce or death without getting too far into the weeds.

Full, up-to-date information is available at *www. socialsecurity.gov*, but like the above quotation taken directly from the website, if you are confused, you are in good company. You can learn more about and/or apply for retirement benefits online, call Social Security at 800-772-1213 (Hint: You could give yourself a complete mani-pedi while you remain on hold), or make an appointment to speak with a representative in person at a local Social Security office.

Your CDFA can flatten out the learning curve by including a discussion of Social Security as part of your overall divorce planning strategy.

IT'S A FACT

Currently, 26.9% of divorced women in America, age 63 and older, are in poverty, as opposed to 11.4% of men. Divorced women receive the lowest average annual Social Security benefit of any group: $10,995.

Source: Ben Steverman, Bloomberg

In General:

- An American who works and pays Social Security taxes qualifies for retirement benefits by earning "credits" toward benefits. Generally, you will need to amass ten years' worth of work credit during which you pay Social Security taxes to qualify.
- Your benefit payment is based on your earnings and the age at which you decide to retire. The retirement age figures have changed, but in

general, you can begin collecting benefits as early as age 62. However, your benefits will be significantly less at that age compared to your full retirement age (approximately 66-67, depending upon the year you were born). Even past that age, benefits increase automatically by a designated percentage until you reach age 70.

- In deciding when to retire and begin collecting benefits, consider that you will need 70-80% of your pre-retirement income to enjoy a comfortable retirement.
- Even if you delay collecting Social Security, you should nevertheless sign up for Medicare (see Chapter 3) at age 65.

After Divorce or Death:

- If you are divorced, but your marriage lasted ten years or longer, you can receive benefits on your ex-spouse's work history record, even if he has remarried, if: 1) you are unmarried; 2) you are age 62 or older; and 3) your ex-spouse is entitled to Social Security and your own benefits would be less than the benefits you would receive based on your ex-spouse's record.
- If you wait to begin collecting your divorced spouse benefits until you reach your full retirement age, you can receive 50% of his benefit. Collecting your benefit does not affect his benefit. In other words, they are not deducting money from his benefit to pay yours.
- If you remarry, you generally cannot collect benefits on your former spouse's record unless your later marriage ends (by death, divorce, or annulment). However, if you remarry at age 60 or over, you will not lose your survivor benefit. You will lose your divorced spouse benefit.

- If your ex-spouse has not applied for retirement benefits, but can qualify for them, you can receive benefits on his record if you have been divorced for at least two years.
- If you are eligible for retirement benefits on your own record and your ex-husband's, Social Security will pay the retirement benefit first. If the benefit on your ex-spouse's record is higher, you will get an additional amount based on your ex-spouse's record so that the combination of benefits equals the higher amount.
- Other factors come into play, including disability and caring for a child who is under age sixteen or disabled.
- When calculating your Social Security benefits, you should note that they may be lower than the stated amount because of Medicare deductions. When you sign up for Medicare at age 65, and are receiving Social Security, your monthly Medicare Part B premium will be deducted automatically from your monthly Social Security payment.

Chapter 3

Medicare

"The older you get, the better you get, unless you're a banana."

— *Betty White*

HEALTHCARE CAN BE THE SECOND-LARGEST expense in a retired person's budget after housing. In contrast to housing costs, which can be somewhat controlled without severe discomfort by downsizing, choosing not to remodel/redecorate, or avoiding/delaying other non-essential projects, healthcare is not only a major expense but the costs tend to increase with age.

Healthcare costs in relation to income typically rise from 10% for people in their fifties to 20% or more for people in their eighties. Medicare was enacted in 1965 to help ameliorate healthcare concerns for seniors. It is a national health insurance program provided to Americans who are 65 and older (as well as to younger people who qualify due to disability or illness). Medicare operates under the Social Security Administration, which is why your

Medicare premium can be deducted from your Social Security benefit.

IT'S A FACT

Nearly half of Americans ages 55-64 believe they will need only $50,000 for healthcare costs in retirement. They wildly underestimate. Typically, a healthy 65-year-old couple will most likely have to pay at least four times that much in medical expenses over the course of their remaining life.

Source: Mature Market Institute, 2011

Oregon Senator Ron Wyden sums up this government program's intent, stating, "The most important aspect of Medicare is…the guarantee to all Americans that they will have high quality healthcare as they get older." That's a laudable aim that the program does, for the most part, deliver on. But Medicare has several elements and different pricing and penalty fees if you don't sign up in time.

I will attempt to make this overview as simple as possible, but remember, we're talking about the United States government. How complex is the program? The 2019 Medicare Handbook produced by the Centers for Medicare & Medicaid Services is filled with jargon that is not always easy to understand. You can find it and other information (such as initial enrollment and open enrollment periods and much more) at *www.medicare.gov.*

Before We Dig In, Please Note:

Unlike Social Security, your Medicare benefits are provided solely to you. They have nothing to do with your marital status or your ex-spouse's benefits.

Notwithstanding the call of some lawmakers for "Medicare for All," universal healthcare is currently a proposal, not a policy. Even if some variation of it were to be signed into law, the program would not take effect soon, and the transition would be measured in years, not months. For now, and into the foreseeable future, Medicare is primarily for Americans age 65 and up.

Starting January 1, 2020, Medigap (Medicare Supplement Insurance) policies sold to new Medicare enrollees will not cover the Part B deductible, meaning Plans C and F will no longer be available to people new to Medicare beginning on that date. People who already have these policies can continue to purchase them if they are available in their location. The general information below is current as of calendar year 2019.

Plans and Premiums

Medicare does not equal healthcare. It is a health insurance program, not a provider of healthcare. In most cases, you can go to any doctor, provider, hospital, or facility enrolled in Medicare and that accepts Medicare patients. Depending upon the provider and the plan you choose, generally, you will have to pay a portion of the cost for each service. Remember, Medicare is not free, although it is far less expensive than healthcare insurance paid by people who are under 65 and not covered by their employer's plan.

Premium-Free Part A

You usually do not pay a monthly premium for Medicare Part A (hospital insurance) coverage if you or your spouse paid Medicare taxes for the required number of years while working. You can get premium-free Part A at age 65 if you are eligible for, or already receive, Social Security benefits.

If you are not eligible for "premium-free" Part A, or you do not sign up when you are first eligible, your monthly premium may go up 10%. You will have to pay the higher premium for twice the number of years you could have had Part A but didn't sign up. Example: If you were eligible for Part A for twelve months but did not sign up, you will pay the penalty for the next twenty-four months.

Part B

You pay a premium each month for Part B (medical insurance). Your Part B premium will be automatically deducted from your Social Security benefit payment if you are currently receiving benefits. If you have opted to wait to sign up for Social Security benefits but are age 65, once you register for Medicare (do this three months before you turn 65), you will be billed for the premium.

If you do not sign up for Part B when you are first eligible, you will pay a fee for as long as you have Part B—it does not go away like the Part A penalty does. The penalty fee is 10% a year. Example: If you sign up for Part B two years after you are eligible, you will pay a 20% penalty each year for as long as you have Medicare Part B.

Part D

Part D is easy to remember: Just think D as in drug coverage. You will pay a monthly premium for Part D along with numerous other things. There is an annual deductible to meet, co-payments, costs in coverage gap… and we cannot forget the penalty for signing up late.

The penalty for Part D is 1% of the "national base

beneficiary premium" ($33.19 in 2019) times the number of full, uncovered months you did not have Part D or creditable coverage. In simple terms, if you sign up twenty months after you are eligible, your late fee will be 20% for as long as you have coverage.

Wait a Minute—Where Is Part C?

A Medicare Advantage Plan is another way to obtain Medicare coverage. These plans—aka Part C—are offered by Medicare-approved private companies that must follow the rules set by Medicare. In most cases, you will be limited to healthcare providers within the plan's network. You will still sign up for Medicare and be billed by Medicare.

Supplemental Coverage

Original Medicare—Parts A, B, and D—will pay for much, but not all, of the cost of covered healthcare services and supplies. "But not all" is the operative phrase here. You can purchase Medicare Supplement Insurance—aka Medigap—policies that offer coverage for services not covered by Original Medicare.

Need More Info?

What we said about Social Security is equally true about Medicare: "It's complicated." In addition to elements such as open enrollment periods, late enrollment penalties, and the array of provider options, there are yearly deductibles, "Extra Help" prescription drug programs, veterans' benefits, employer/union coverage issues…and on and on.

California residents can call the California Health Insurance Counseling & Advocacy Program (HICAP) at 800-434-0222 to obtain free, personalized health insurance counseling or Medicare at 800-633-4227 to get answers to general questions and help choosing the coverage option best for them. HMOs and PPOs can give you specific details on their programs. A comprehensive Medicare Handbook is sent via snail mail or email to each recipient annually. In addition to explaining how to sign up for Medicare and describing the various options, it offers charts that enable you to compare health and prescription drug plans in your area.

The beauty of Medicare is that each year during the open enrollment period from October 15 through December 7, you have an opportunity to change your coverage for the following year. So, unlike some financial decisions that have permanent consequences, Medicare makes accommodations for your changing needs.

Chapter 4

Risk Tolerance

"The trouble is, if you don't risk anything, you risk even more."

— Erica Jong

THERE IS NOTHING WRONG WITH being the person who wants to ride the rapids, scale the heights, or jump out of a perfectly good airplane. There is nothing wrong with being the person who prefers to watch these escapades from the comfort of their couch.

We all take risks when we go about our daily routine; getting into a car is so much a part of our life that we seldom think about potential mishaps—or worse. We take risks when we make major decisions such as buying a home, embarking on a new job, or getting married.

Some risks are unavoidable; some are avoidable. Each of us has a risk-taking comfort level.

Calculating your risk tolerance is a prelude to investing, which is why we are tackling the topic in this chapter. Your tolerance dictates how much risk you as an investor are willing to take in hopes of a gain and how much you are willing to lose if your investments do poorly. Just as getting married means taking a big risk, the art of divorce bargaining involves risk tolerance as well.

Whether investing in stocks and bonds or negotiating a divorce, you will be best served by deeply contemplating the level of risk with which you are comfortable. You can find risk tolerance questionnaires online. They may be a good starting point, but as with a health-screening questionnaire, you need an adept professional to help you work through the process, tally the results, understand the results, and find a path forward that works for you.

As a CDFA, I address the concept with you as it pertains to your divorce and your investments. We consider how much risk you can and should take based on your age, investment durations, and other elements. We discuss how much risk you might have to take to reach your goals, and if your tolerance and goals don't mesh, how you might have to adjust your goals.

Even for the most risk-averse person, the biggest risk lies in not doing what is necessary to achieve your long-term financial goals.

Factors to Consider

As with every activity, risk happens. Whether you are investing your heart or your money, the investment may pay off or it may cost you. When it comes to financial investments, you should consider the following factors:

- **Your age.** The younger you are, the more risky and frisky you can be. You'll have more time to recover from a financial setback at age 35 than you will at age 60.
- **Your diversification strategy.** If you have a wide array of investments, plus readily available cash,

your overall, lower-risk situation will allow you to jump on riskier opportunities, assuming they fit within your comfort level.

- **Your financial IQ.** If you do not know much about investing, you will not have the knowledge, understanding, or confidence to make decisions—especially about higher-risk investments. Having a skilled financial advisor as your partner is critical. You need someone you can trust to provide sound advice customized to your needs and comfort level and upon whom you can rely to guide you to products that will benefit you, not themselves.

An Archaeological Dig into Your Deepest Self

To understand your risk tolerance, you will need to think deeply about your personal investment philosophy, your comfort level with fluctuations caused by things outside your control (such as inflation, interest rates, or trade wars), the trade-offs between potential returns and declines, and the like.

Risk tolerance questions delve into the core of your being. Remember: No answer is right or wrong; they simply reflect who you are.

Some questionnaires ask the potential investor how they would react if the value of their portfolio plunged 25% or more in one year. What would you do? A lower-risk-tolerant, conservative investor would typically react by moving their money to "safer" investments even if they might miss out on a potential recovery. Someone with moderate risk tolerance would leave their money where it is in accordance with their long-term financial investment strategy. A higher-risk-tolerant, aggressive investor would be chomping at the bit to seize the opportunity to invest even more money.

Risks and Rewards

SIDEBAR

"Zero risk" does not exist in life or investments. When it comes to investing, risk is the chance you take. The higher the risk, the more you can gain…but the more you might lose. The lower the risk, the less you can gain…but the less you might lose.

Lower-risk investments include treasury bonds, money market funds, and certificates of deposit (CDs). Going up the risk ladder, limited-risk investments include blue chip stocks, high yield municipal or corporate bonds, and mutual funds. Moderate-risk investors will consider putting their money into growth stocks, B-rated corporate bonds, and international investments. High-risk, high-reward-seeking individuals may invest in futures, speculative stocks, and high-yield bonds.

As you will learn in Chapter 5, two keys factors of a comprehensive investment strategy are: 1) diversifying your investments so you have a variety of varying risk level assets; and 2) crafting a strategy to plan your portfolio. In other words, you do not want to put all your (nest) eggs in one basket, and you need to start with a good, strong basket.

To put risk vs. reward in perspective, let's go shopping! At Nordstrom—for Christian Louboutin heels. If I am working with a woman who is nervous about investing because the market is down, I offer this analogy:

> You see a pair of shoes you lust after. You try them on. You adore them. But they're $800, so you de-

cide not to buy them. You go home and obsess over them for three weeks. You return to the store. They're still there! And now they're on sale for $500. Do you say, "Oh, I think I'll wait until they go back up to full price?" Of course not. You buy them immediately.

All investing involves risk, including loss of principal. No strategy ensures success or protects against loss. There is no guarantee that a diversified portfolio will enhance overall returns or outperform a non-diversified portfolio. Diversification does not protect against market risk.

Chapter 5

Investing

"You have brains in your head. You have feet in your shoes. You can steer yourself any direction you choose. You're on your own. And you know what you know. And YOU are the one who'll decide where to go."

— *Dr. Seuss*

CHECK YOUR WALLET, YOUR PURSE, your pockets, or peek under the couch cushions and you'll find it. Cash. We all have money. However, how much we know about making it work for us in the short- and long-term differs widely from person to person.

The venerable *Wall Street Journal* has published a 150-page "Guide to Understanding Money & Investing." Investment firms and professionals immersed in the field have written articles, blogs, essays, books, and voluminous tomes on saving and investing. I do not attempt in this book to replicate these sources, but to provide an easy-to-comprehend overview to familiarize you with financial vehicles.

My intent is to introduce you to the challenges and opportunities involved in investing, to describe basic products, and to help you forge a path forward. Some people go it alone, but most people choose a financial advisor to help them manage their wealth—at whatever level that "wealth" might be.

Even if you work with a professional broker to manage the brokerage account in which you buy, hold, and sell your investments, the more you know about these tools, the more confident and capable you will be. I want to empower you to act not as a passive but active partner in this journey.

Think of it like sailing on a ship: You don't need to know how every piece of equipment works, but you do want to know where you're going, how you'll get there, and when you'll arrive.

If divorce is in your future, you need to know the worth of your current investments so you can make an equitable division of those assets. If your spouse has died, or has a terminal illness, you also need to know these things. Once you are single, either through divorce or death, you need to be able to move forward on your own.

Investments:
- Checking and Savings—safe, low to no return on investment (ROI)
- Certificate of deposit—safe, relatively low ROI over fixed period
- Stocks—more risk of losing money, potential for high return
- Bonds—typically safer, lower yield than stocks; company is borrowing money from you
- Mutual Funds—buying into sets of stocks and/or bonds
- Annuities—paying over time in exchange for guaranteed income later

Checking and Savings Accounts

Your relationship with money dates back to your childhood. You probably conducted your initial financial transactions while in elementary school, when your parents gave you an allowance. Your piggy bank represented a savings account into which you could dip to buy extras like an ice cream cone or a comic book. Today, your life has become more complex, but the notion of putting money aside for future use remains the same.

Most people maintain personal accounts at a bank or credit union. Checking accounts typically pay no interest; in fact, you often pay the institution a monthly maintenance fee. You also may be charged a fee for a savings account, but you do receive a (low) rate of interest on the balance.

CDs

A Certificate of Deposit (CD) is a vehicle with a fixed interest rate and a fixed time limit, typically, from three months to several years. The interest rate rises in accordance with the certificate's duration.

Generally, you earn more interest on a CD as opposed to a savings account because the financial institution will enjoy the use of your money for a defined period. You can withdraw money from your savings account whenever you want without a penalty. If you cash in your CD before it matures, you will pay a penalty (usually in the form of forfeited interest). Remember the old warning, "There may be substantial penalties for early withdrawal."

Although CDs seem like a safe way to make money, the truth is that you may actually lose buying power if: 1) the CD offers 3% interest over four years; 2) you are in the 20% tax bracket; and 3) inflation is 2%.

To put it in dollars and sense (and jewelry!), let's say the Cartier bracelet you want to buy costs $2,000 today. You have $2,000 in a CD that will mature in three years.

Choosing Your Best Fitting Fund

We'll say you want to invest in a large-growth mutual fund. All funds do not fit alike, so how can you know which one will fit best? One of the more popular research firms is Morningstar® (*www.morningstar.com*). Morningstar is an investment research firm that compiles and analyzes mutual fund data. The Morningstar rating provides a measure of a fund's risk-adjusted return relative to similar

SIDEBAR

funds. Funds are rated from one to five stars, with the best performers receiving five stars and the worst a single star.

Advantages of Dollar-Cost Averaging

Many investors regard dollar-cost averaging as a lower-risk, stress-free way to participate in the market. The strategy makes market volatility less of an issue and puts you on a routine that you do not need to think or worry about.

Instead of investing a lump sum of money, you would establish a plan to have a fixed amount of money withdrawn from your checking account at monthly (or other) intervals to invest in shares of a mutual fund. By setting aside this fixed sum, regardless of the fluctuating price per share, you spread out the cost and insulate yourself against changes in market prices. By removing emotion from the process, you end up buying more shares when the price is lower without trying to "game" the market.

Example of dollar-cost averaging

	Amount Invested	Price Per Share	Shares Purchased
April	$100	$10	10
May	$100	$15	6.7
June	$100	$13	7.7
TOTAL	$300	$12.67* $12.32**	24.4

* $12.67 is the average price per share
** $12.32 is the average cost per share using dollar-cost averaging

This is a hypothetical example and not representative of any specific investment. Your results may vary.

As you can see from the chart, dollar-cost averaging works best when you: 1) can afford to keep your interval investment consistent; 2) invest in a vehicle you plan to hold for five years or longer; and 3) combine this program with diversification and other strategies.

Annuity

An annuity is an investment vehicle backed by an insurance company that pays a guaranteed stream of income. Historically, annuities were primarily used as an income stream for retirees.

In the old days, you put your money in a fixed annuity so you would be guaranteed an income stream later in life. Insurance companies used an actuary table to guess how long you would live. Then they divided the amount of money in the annuity by the number of years and came up with a dollar amount. They guaranteed you that amount of income every year until you died. If you passed away before that specific date, the insurance company kept the "left-over" money. If you lived beyond their determined number of years, they had to continue paying you the income...ouch to them.

Today, annuities have become much more complex. You can invest in an annuity. You can choose to buy mutual funds within the annuity, including large-growth, small-growth, international, and even bond funds.

As you can see from this graph, one of the many advantages of investing in annuities is the money grows tax-free.

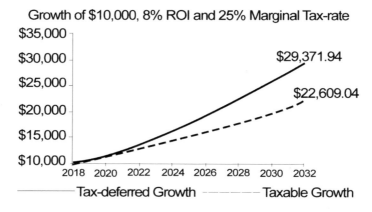

Growth of $10,000, 8% ROI and 25% Marginal Tax-rate

This is a hypothetical example and not representative of any specific investment. Your results may vary.

How to Use an Annuity

Why should you invest in an annuity? It may be a viable way to save and earn for the future. If your ex-husband pays you monthly spousal support, you can take a portion of that money and invest in an annuity. Down the road, when he is no longer obligated to pay support, you can activate the annuity to continue your guaranteed stream of income over the rest of your life.

Decisions, Decisions, Decisions

As you can see, there are many types of investment vehicles from which to choose, so choose wisely and well.

Take it from Apple, Inc. co-founder Steve Jobs, who noted, "Deciding what not to do is as important as deciding what to do." Trust in a skilled financial advisor to help you chart your path.

CDs are FDIC Insured to specific limits and offer a fixed rate of return if held to maturity. Bonds are subject to market and interest rate risk if sold prior to maturity. Bond values will decline as interest rates rise, and bonds are subject to availability and change in price.

Dollar-cost averaging involves continued investment in securities regardless of fluctuation in price levels of such securities. An investor should consider their ability to continue purchasing through fluctuating price levels. Such a plan does not assure a profit and does not protect against loss in declining markets. All investing involves risk, including loss of principal.

Fixed and Variable annuities are suitable for long-term investing, such as retirement investing. Gains from tax-deferred investments are taxable as ordinary income upon withdrawal. Guarantees are based on the claims-paying ability of the issuing company. Withdrawals made prior to age 59½ are subject to a 10% IRS penalty tax and surrender charges may apply. Variable annuities are subject to market risk and may lose value.

Chapter 6

Credit

"Money is only a tool. It will take you
wherever you wish, but it will not replace you
as the driver."

— Ayn Rand

CREDIT CARD DEBT IS UNSECURED debt, meaning that it is not attached to a specific asset, such as a car, which the lender can retrieve if the debt is not paid. If you have multiple cards and maintain high balances on them, the debt can be substantial and is generally exacerbated by high interest rates.

Like your good name, good credit is a valuable asset that must be protected during and after a divorce or upon the death of a spouse. To get started, you should request your annual free copy of all three credit bureau reports (Experian, Equifax, and Transunion) at *www.annualcred-itreport.com.* That way, you can ascertain your credit score and inventory all accounts that are open jointly or in your own name.

If you are divorcing/divorced, you should close all joint credit accounts and transition to single accounts so your ex-husband's credit score will not affect yours. If your spouse dies, you are responsible for paying the deceased spouse's bills, even if the cards are in his name alone.

Divorce negotiations need to include a discussion of who gets which card(s). The optimum solution would be to pay in full all joint accounts and then close them. You can then choose to open new accounts in your own name.

If closing these accounts is not feasible, you should make sure you have full control of the ones divided as part of the settlement. This must be made crystal clear in the divorce decree, which will state that you are liable for this account and will hold your spouse "harmless" from having to pay the debt and vice-versa. The decree should also state the specific dollar amount owed on the card at the time of divorce.

Spouse alert: Determine if either of you is a signatory on an account, as opposed to jointly liable. If the credit card is based on the joint income of both spouses, it is a joint debt. If the card is in one name only with the second person granted signatory rights, the second spouse may not be jointly liable. This varies from state to state. When in doubt, contact the credit card company yourself.

Credit Scores: What They Are and Why They Matter

Aside from bragging rights, credit scores are significant. Just as a high GPA helps a student get accepted into a good university, a high credit score gives you access to more of the good things in life—and often at a lower cost, to boot.

Lenders use credit scores to guide them in deciding whether or not to offer you credit and at what rate. Lenders see higher scores as representing prudent credit decisions, thus making them more confident that you will repay future debt.

If you are buying a home or car, a higher score can yield a lower interest rate, meaning you could save hundreds—even thousands—of dollars over the course of a loan. If you are suddenly single, having a good credit score can help you qualify for an apartment lease to tide you over while deciding what to do next.

Find Your FICO

A majority of lenders look at FICO scores, created by the Fair Isaac Corporation. These scores generally range from 300-850. The higher the score, the more attractive you are to lenders.

The majority of credit scores range from 600-750. Lenders typically consider a FICO above 670-700 as a good credit score, and 800 or more as exceptional. If your credit score soars near the magic 850 mark, lenders may roll out the red carpet and throw loans at your feet.

IT'S A FACT

To maintain a higher credit score, limit your use of available credit, especially on revolving credit cards. The less available credit you use, the better: 30% or less is good; 20% or less is better; 10% or less is best. This equation applies even if you pay off your balances in full every month (which you should strive to do) since credit bureaus use statement balances to calculate your scores.

You Can Improve Your Scores

Unlike a child's report card ("Little Bailey met the first-grade academic standards, but behavior needs improvement!"), your credit scores are not stored in your credit history until the end of time. Your score is generated every time it is requested by a lender, giving you an opportunity to increase it by making wise decisions when using plastic and paying the bills.

Many factors affect the scores in your credit report. Among them are: 1) payment history, in particular, the number and severity of late payments; 2) the number and longevity of credit accounts; 3) how much you charge on each account and the percentage of that amount paid each month; 4) total debt and your debt-to-income ratio; 5) negative marks resulting from a foreclosure or bankruptcy.

When you examine your credit reports meticulously, detail by detail, you can understand and modify activities that negatively affect your scores while boosting activities that raise your score. You also can add a brief statement explaining a negative notation.

If your ex has already drug your credit score through the mud and your credit score is less than the cost of a latte, you might want to improve your FICO score and repair the damage.

Chapter 7

Financial Planning

"Pour yourself a drink, put on some lipstick,
and pull yourself together."

— *Elizabeth Taylor*

A<small>S SOMEONE WHO NOT ONLY</small> has been a financial advisor for twenty-five-plus years but also a woman who waited until I was forty-five to marry Mr. Right (and John is exactly that!), I understand the nuances of financial planning—including creating and adhering to a budget—from both a professional and personal perspective.

It is my mission to help women who may not have "been there, done that" tackle this new chapter in their life. Part of financial planning is simple math: making the numbers add up. But before you can do that, you need to take a deep dive into what you absolutely need and what you want, so you can craft a realistic budget. After you have your budget in place comes the next challenge: sticking to it.

As with everything else today, from fresh lemonade recipes to 3D printing of a mechanical hummingbird, you can find budgeting worksheets, tips, and apps on the Internet. These can be useful research tools, but your money is too vital to your lifestyle to trust to a so-called expert on the Internet. I strongly advise you to consult with a financial professional in person to help you prepare a budget that works for you.

The Prelude: Your Financial Statement

As part of your divorce, most states have a standard Financial Affidavit form that both parties must complete. This sworn, notarized statement will be part of your recorded divorce documents filed with the court.

In the statement, you and your spouse will itemize expenses such as home, food, childcare, entertainment, medical, insurance, vehicle, clothing, and the like. That is "where the money goes." You will also list "where the money comes from," as in employment, Social Security, and other sources.

This financial affidavit is a good place for you to begin as you move forward in singlehood. Whether you are emerging on the other side of a divorce or a death, you need to keep your emotions out of your plan. Denying your reduced circumstances, resenting your spouse's decision to divorce and leave you adrift, and/ or being fearful of how you'll manage are all normal emotions, but they are negative, not positive. Send your denial, anger, and fear on a long walk on the proverbial short pier, and watch them fall and sink into the water so you can move on.

Some municipalities and businesses have evolved to a zero-based budget. Instead of relying on the past fiscal year's budget to plan for the following year (oh, we spent $X on lightbulbs and $X on marketing materials last year, so let's just add 5% to those costs), each line item begins at zero. Each expenditure must be validated as necessary before it is included.

This approach might work well for women making a fresh start—so will a realistic attitude that doesn't leave you feeling defeated, but energized. Recognize that some expenses may be easy and relatively painless to modify. No need to kiss your housekeeper goodbye. Instead of bringing someone in once a week, how about once a month? Do you need a mani-pedi every two weeks, or could you stretch it out a bit? Instead of dining out three times per week, eat at home and treat yourself to a good bottle of wine.

On Your Mark, Get Set, Go: Let's Create Your Budget!

Ready to start planning for the rest of your life? Let's get started. Here are some simple steps you can take. Remember, there is no need to be fancy. You can use an Excel spreadsheet, a Word document, or just a pencil and lined paper. The important thing is to get going on it.

1. Write down your financial goals. What are your priorities? Putting aside money for emergencies? Taking one or two trips a year? Saving up to buy a new car in three years?

2. Write down your monthly net income; include all revenue coming in.

3. Write down your monthly expenses. Some expenditures for recurring items such as utilities and cable are fairly standard and need to be paid every month. Some, such as property taxes, dental visits, and car and home insurance, occur periodically. You will want to add all of these up and divide by twelve so you can calculate your monthly expenditures. Your expenses can be categorized as fixed (such as your mortgage payment) and variable (such as food, clothing, and entertainment). Reducing fixed expenses is not easy, but it

is possible; for example, you could downsize your cellphone/cable plans. Adjusting variable expenses is doable and may be advisable.

4. Make sure you set aside as much money as you can in savings and/or investment accounts for that rainy day you think will never come but will—probably when you least expect it.

5. After you meticulously document every expenditure for three months, making sure you document each and every transaction for all of your accounts, review your budget. Did you have surprise expenses such as an unplanned doctor's visit, a quick trip out of town, or an impulse buy?

6. If you are coming up short, do a little more soul-searching and decide what adjustments you can make. Then make them. Perhaps you can get a part-time job to help fund your requirements. Perhaps you can pare down a bit more.

7. Your budget is a work in progress. Review and revise it as needed.

8. Make it fun! Challenge yourself to live below your means. Look for restaurant coupons and good CD rates, and think about making minor changes that add up to major savings.

Chapter 8

Child Support vs. Alimony

"Married in haste, we may repent at leisure."
— *William Congreve*

CHILD SUPPORT VS. ALIMONY: THAT is the question. The answer lies in your needs, your children's needs, and the respective tax burdens.

The quote at the top of this chapter, which has evolved into an everyday adage, applies not only to a marriage but to an improper structuring of the divorce settlement (as does another saying: Haste makes waste).

This is a case where you really need to do your homework, optimally, before negotiations begin. Even if you and your husband are engaging in a "friendly" divorce with the use of a mediator, you (and he) need to know each (ex)spouse's rights, obligations, and tax consequences.

Attorneys, financial planners, and accountants (even CPAs), although they excel in their field, often do not know the intricacies and potential complications related to child support and spousal support, aka alimony. A CDFA has a depth and breadth of knowledge that can make the difference between you experiencing a good life for you and your children or repenting at leisure.

The subject is complex. The following discussion offers a basic overview. For more information, I strongly advise you to seek out a Certified Divorce Financial Analyst who has the knowledge and expertise to guide you to make the best decisions.

IT'S A FACT

Regardless of marital status, parents are obligated to support their children until they turn eighteen.

Child Support Guidelines

After a divorce, the non-custodial parent (assuming there is no joint custody agreement) is typically ordered by the judge to pay a designated amount of child support monthly to the custodial parent. This money is intended to be used by the custodial parent to pay the child's expenses, not her own.

Among the numerous elements factored into the equation are the number of children; the income of the non-custodial parent; whether that parent is paying separately for childcare, health insurance, and/or education expenses; and the percentage of time each child resides with that parent.

In our American judicial system, the courts strive mightily to protect the children of divorce. Once the amount of child support has been set by the court, it can be modified only when a substantial change in circumstances occurs and only when agreed to by the court. In other words, a non-custodial father cannot wake up one morning and decide, "Well, since the kids are going to spend winter break with me, I don't need to pay my ex-wife child support for the next month."

Tax Regulations

Child support payments cannot be deducted by the ex-spouse who makes the payments. They are not reported as income by the ex-spouse who receives the payments on behalf of the child(ren).

Another important consideration is the tax exemption. In any given year, the child can be claimed as an exemption for tax purposes by only one parent. The custodial parent generally can claim the child as an exemption. To trade the exemption year to year requires a written waiver or IRS Form 8332.

Is Alimony Taxable?

The answer to this question is yes. Unless otherwise designated, spousal support is taxable to the recipient and deductible to the payer. In some cases, depending upon circumstances and the marital settlement agreement, both spouses can agree that all or part of the spousal support payments will be treated as both non-taxable to the recipient and non-deductible to the payer. This language must be clearly and unambiguously stated in the agreement so that the IRS does not come knocking at your door.

Spousal support involves other tax considerations. You need to know the tax consequences of receiving alimony monthly or as a lump sum.

More About Alimony

In the case of gray divorces, the kids are usually over eighteen, which makes child support vs. alimony a moot point. Depending upon the state in which you live and your and your husband's financial situation (e.g., perhaps he is self-employed with an income that fluctuates from month to month), alimony takes several forms. In addition to the monthly or lump sum variety, you may be eligible to receive temporary alimony (interim support paid for a defined time while the divorce is pending or until the receiving spouse becomes eligible for Social Security), rehabilitative alimony (to help the receiving spouse gain education/training to attain financial independence), or reimbursement alimony (when one spouse has supported the other's education).

In California, a marriage lasting at least ten years is considered to be a long-term marriage and threshold for alimony. Typically, alimony does not last forever (although it may seem to, for the complaining ex). The IRS requires that it end upon the death of the receiving spouse (a no-brainer). It often ends upon that person's remarriage, or in some cases, cohabitation. It also may be modified or terminated in certain situations.

A Note of Caution: If you will be receiving alimony for an extended period of time, you might want to have a guarantee in place that the payments will continue if something such as disability, serious illness, or death should befall the paying spouse. This guarantee could take the form of life insurance or disability insurance in an appropriate amount to replace the monetary value of the alimony payments.

Chapter 9

Get Your Fair Share of His Retirement Benefits

"All's fair in love and war."

— *Proverb*

"All's fair in love, war, and divorce."

— *Deana Carter*

DEFINED BENEFIT PLANS, COMMONLY KNOWN as pension plans, have gone the way of poodle skirts and princess telephones. Most have been replaced by Defined Contribution Plans such as a 401(k).

Nevertheless, pensions continue to exist in the public sector, so if your spouse served in the military or works/worked for local, state, or federal government, he probably receives a pension. He may have been in an industry that provided a traditional plan in which the employer made all contributions. Employees also may have paid a sum allocated from their monthly salary.

After a designated period, the employees become vested, which means they are eligible for pension benefits upon retirement. They can choose the type of payout: 1) lump sum, or 2) pension annuity. The latter provides regular payments for as long as the person (and, in some cases, the spouse) lives.

IT'S A FACT

Although a pension guarantees the retiree a specific dollar amount, most pensions are not adjusted for inflation, meaning the fixed amount received will buy less with each passing year.

How can you make sure to get your portion of his retirement? And what are the tax consequences?

First, let's look at the other side of the retirement coin: Defined Contribution Plans. Whereas a Defined Benefit Plan guarantees the recipient a specific amount of money when the person retires (based on salary and/or length of service), a defined contribution plan does not provide a guaranteed benefit amount. Factors affecting the benefit include the amount contributed prior to retirement, the plan's management, and overall economic conditions.

Today, the most common defined contribution plan, and indeed, the most common retirement vehicle, is the 401(k). In this plan, employees contribute pre-tax dollars via payroll deduction. The taxes will be paid when the benefits are distributed. In some cases, employers contribute as well.

With these types of plans, you can roll over your share into another qualified retirement plan or Individual Retirement Account (IRA) so it can continue growing on a tax-deferred basis. If you do not roll over the entire amount, you must pay taxes on the amount you did not roll over or face taxes and penalties.

There are also other types of retirement plans. For instance, if one of you is self-employed, you might have a Simplified Employee Pension Plan, commonly known as a SEP IRA. The important point to note is that whatever the plan, it may be subject to division during divorce proceedings.

A Rollover Can Be a Taxing Situation

Be mindful when taking money from your spouse's retirement plan(s). Your financial advisor can fill you in on the details, but in brief, if you think you might need some of your ex-spouse's money for divorce-related or other expenses, you may not want to roll over all of the funds into an IRA.

If assets from your husband's 401(k) are allocated in your settlement under a Qualified Domestic Relations Order (QDRO), you are allowed to make a one-time withdrawal before rolling over the remaining money into an IRA. You will *not* have to pay the IRS a 10% penalty for early withdrawal, even if you are under age 59½. You *will* have to report and pay income taxes on the amount of money withdrawn (unless the funds were specified as a ROTH 401(k) contribution).

To put this in context, let's say your portion of your ex's 401(k) is $50,000. You decide to roll $40,000 of that money into an IRA so that you will not pay penalty or tax on that amount. You decide to withdraw and spend

$10,000 fixing up the house, getting cosmetic surgery, or dashing to Aruba with your hot new boy toy. You will not have to pay a penalty, but you will have to pay income tax on the $10,000.

Remember: This is a one-time-only withdrawal opportunity. Should you roll over the entire $50,000 into an IRA, then later decide to withdraw $10,000, you will be subject to a 10% early withdrawal fee if you are under 59½.

Military Retirements

If your spouse was or still is in the military, special considerations apply. In general, you as the former spouse are eligible for a portion of his disposable retirement pay. The situation is complex, so you need to determine his earnings.

If he is currently serving, get a copy of the Leave and Earnings Statement (LES). This voucher explains what he is paid, what the deductions are, and what elective allotments are in place. If he is retired, get a copy of the Retiree Account Statement (RAS), so you will be able to value and divide this asset.

Looking Ahead: RMDs

If you think Social Security and Medicare are complicated, just wait until you get close to 70½ years old. That is the age at which you must begin taking minimum distributions from certain retirement accounts. To make something complicated nearly incomprehensible, in the first year, you must take one Required Minimum Distribution (RMD) by April 1 following the year you reach 70½, then a second RMD by that year's end. After that, you must withdraw one RMD each year by December 31.

Why does the IRS want you to deplete your savings—and at a higher rate each year? Because the money you are withdrawing was tax-deferred savings and now each RMD will be subject to ordinary income taxes—the government wants their money.

In general, retirement accounts subject to RMD regulations include 401(k), 403(b), Keogh qualified plans, traditional and simple IRAs, and SEPs.

Roth IRAs are not subject to RMD rules. If your husband owns a Roth IRA and you are the sole beneficiary, if he dies, you become the new owner. In this situation, the IRS allows a spousal rollover and does not require distributions to be made (or taxed).

You Have Only One Chance to Get Your QDRO Right

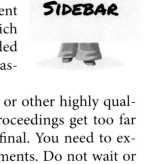

SIDEBAR

A Qualified Domestic Relations Order (QDRO) is a legal order from the court to the retirement plan administrator. It precisely defines and quantifies the plan's benefits as they will be assigned to each party in a divorce. Most, but not all, retirement plans are divisible by a QDRO, which states how the money will be divided now, plus what will happen to the assets if/when one of the parties dies.

You must consult with a CDFA or other highly qualified financial advisor before the proceedings get too far and certainly before the divorce is final. You need to examine the applicable pension documents. Do not wait or you could lose this valuable asset!

As stated in *Financial Issues of Divorce*, written by the Institute for Divorce Financial Analysts (the organization that grants CDFA certification):

There are too many horror stories where the [divorce] case has gone to court, everything is settled, and the judge says the divorce is final and that a QDRO should be drafted to give the ex-spouse her half of the pension as a lump sum. The QDRO is sent to the pension plan and the ex-spouse ends up not getting any of the plan money. Why? Because the plan does not have to pay a lump sum and will not pay any of the benefits to the spouse.

Do not let this happen to you!

Chapter 10

Health Equals Wealth

"A woman is like a tea bag; you never know
how strong it is until it's in hot water."

— Eleanor Roosevelt

I N 2018, AMERICANS BORROWED MORE than $88 billion to pay health expenses. This chapter and the next two are three sides of the healthcare coin. (Oh, wait, a coin has only two sides…well, you get the idea).

Health really does equal wealth in the most fundamental sense. Therefore, it is vital that you proactively protect your health financially just as you protect it physically by getting annual mammograms and other key exams and by taking care of your body, mind, and spirit.

Even the most amicable of divorces is stressful. Most proceedings are far from friendly at the conclusion, even if they commence with that laudable goal.

If you are overeating, undereating, not getting enough exercise, sleeping poorly, drinking too much, or exhibiting other symptoms of stress and anxiety, now would be a great time to schedule a wellness checkup with your primary care physician. You also should conduct a health insurance checkup to ascertain financial wellness.

Research Your Health Insurance Needs

If you have been covered under your husband's health insurance policy, be aware that after your divorce or upon his death, you may face a big gap in coverage before you are eligible for Medicare at age 65.

Currently, if you do not have your own health insurance through your employer, you can maintain coverage after spousal divorce/death for up to thirty-six months through the federal Consolidated Omnibus Budget Reconciliation Act (COBRA)...as long as you pay the premiums.

The problem (and it's a big one) is that the premium cost will be a lot (a LOT) more than pre-divorce—as much as 102% of the cost of the plan. So, the aptly named COBRA slithers along for three years, but in the meantime, it can strangle your bank account.

You do have other options. If you obtain a job with health insurance, you can breathe easier. If you are not working or are self-employed, you should investigate and evaluate your options, including individual and group plans, and health exchanges that operate under the Affordable Care Act.

The next two chapters continue the healthcare conversation as you move into your later years, but take note: First, you need to navigate successfully and healthfully through the here and now.

Chapter 11

Long-Term Care Insurance

*"I'm not afraid of death; I just don't want to be
there when it happens."*

— *Woody Allen*

ALTHOUGH SEVEN OUT OF TEN people over age 65
will need Long-Term Care (LTC) at some point,
fewer than one out of five baby boomers plan for these
needs. These sobering statistics come from a Nationwide®
Financial info-sheet on Long-Term Care.

LTC refers to expenses covering people who have
been certified as chronically ill and/or afflicted with cog-
nitive impairment. It can be provided on an outpatient or
inpatient basis.

The three LTC categories are: 1) home healthcare; 2)
assisted living care; and 3) nursing home care. The total LTC cost over one person's lifetime typically exceeds
$200,000. Who will pay for this, and how will it be paid?

Medicare support, which is limited to 100 days in a
nursing home, does not pay for conditions diagnosed as

LTC. Medicaid, a government program, covers LTC costs, but only for people who are at or below designated poverty levels. Medicaid currently covers six out of ten nursing home residents. Some of these people were middle or even upper class before being hit with a severe health crisis or chronic illness.

So, no matter what your current level of wealth, you need to think ahead and plan for long-term care. Your CDFA can help you make a wise choice on LTC as part of your overall financial strategy.

A Cautionary Tale

Beware of heady promises from LTC insurance providers. In the July 28, 2019, *Los Angeles Times*, reporter Michael Hiltzik shared the saga of an insurance broker who sold LTC policies and bought one for himself and his wife. The broker was blindsided when the life insurance company jacked up its monthly premiums by 80%. If the couple did not pay this exorbitant increase, their future daily benefits would decrease considerably. If they closed the policy, they would lose the substantial amount of money they had invested. At the time this article was written, the couple was deciding on whether to accept the huge increase in premiums or the huge decrease in coverage. Many aging adults with limited financial resources are forced to choose the latter.

Many LTC policies were sold to baby boomers in the 1990s. The pitch was that long-term care can be outrageously expensive, which is true—as much as $100,000 or more per year. Without this policy, it was argued, people needing care at the end of their lives would be forced to rely on Medicaid.

During the LTC heyday, hundreds of companies sold millions of policies. In 2018, about one dozen insurers sold 57,000 policies, with more reasonable benefits than earlier versions. Many of the "bad apples" have disappeared, meaning that the companies still in the game are more trustworthy.

Options Abound; Choose Wisely and Live Well

If you find yourself suddenly single due to divorce or death, you will want to protect your retirement savings from the potentially devastating financial expenses of long-term care. One way to do this is by purchasing a universal life insurance policy or an annuity with an optional LTC benefit rider. Once set, your policy costs will not increase as long as you pay your premiums and fulfill other requirements. In other words, you will possess a policy that combines guaranteed LTC benefits with guaranteed life insurance or annuity benefits for a guaranteed premium.

A linked life insurance policy from a reputable company will provide tax-free LTC insurance if you need it and life insurance benefits for your heirs if you don't. It also provides a money-back guarantee should you change your mind. This type of contract is usually funded with a one-time payment; in other words, you do not pay ongoing premiums. This "hybrid" is viable for people who can move an asset not needed for their retirement income into the policy.

An important caveat is that the person may have to qualify based on health history. For instance, someone who has suffered two heart attacks and a stroke probably will not qualify for a life insurance policy with LTC benefits, but they may still be able to purchase an annuity with LTC benefits.

I have seen the results of not planning ahead for long-term care, and it is not a pretty sight. Without LTC insurance, even relatively affluent individuals can burn through substantial savings built up over a lifetime and still end up on Medicaid. An LTC policy can help you remain independent while not burdening your family with caregiving.

Chapter 12

Life Insurance

"Needing insurance is like needing a parachute: if it isn't there the first time, chances are you won't be needing it again."

— *Author Unknown*

LIFE INSURANCE IS A MAJOR part of the divorce settlement, and you need to lock it in at the beginning of negotiations. Life insurance is used to cover the gap if your spouse were to expire before he is done paying alimony, child support, or your Neiman Marcus bill. If you have children hoping to attend Yale or USC, an adequate death benefit would certainly come in handy to cover tuition—and the Versace you wish to wear to their graduation.

It is vital to get your soon-to-be-ex approved for life insurance before the divorce is final. If, due to medical conditions, he is not insurable or must pay a higher premium, you want to know before an agreement is reached so the settlement can be adjusted.

Equally important, you need to make sure: 1) you are the owner of the policy; and 2) he is responsible for premium payments. Your policy ownership makes it impossible for him to change the beneficiary to his new "Bambi." If he fails to make a payment, you as the owner will be notified.

Ownership also protects you. If he cancelled the policy and then died, you would be, as they say, screwed. Speaking of hubby deaths, typically, a newly widowed woman's expenses decrease by about 20%, but her income may decrease as much as 50%, so having life insurance is the best policy.

One reason I became a Certified Divorce Financial Analyst was precisely so I could help divorcing women handle these financial concerns. Often, a non-CDFA may not understand the importance of making you—as the recipient of spousal and/or child support—the owner of the life insurance contract. But it is a critical element of your financial security.

Types of Life Insurance

As a non-liquid asset, life insurance cannot be easily transformed into cash, but as you now know, this asset is definitely valuable. Different types of policies have differing cash surrenders and other values. In brief, here are two common types:

1. **Term:** Sometimes known as "pure" insurance, a term insurance policy pays upon death. Since it does not accumulate any cash value, term insurance is less expensive than other types. But it only lasts for a given term, and as Shakespeare said (not about life insurance, but about life), "There's the rub." Nearly nine out of ten people outlive their term insurance. Does the nice insurance company refund their money? Is the sky green with purple polka dots? Using the analogy of car insurance, let's say you insure your Mercedes to

the max for five years without once needing to access the insurance to cover any damages. Then you sell the car. Does the nice insurance company refund your five years' worth of money? Is the sky purple with green polka dots?

2. **Permanent:** In contrast to term insurance, a permanent policy does accumulate a cash value that you can borrow against. A portion of your premium will be invested in a fund that earns tax-deferred interest (unless/until you withdraw it), and the policy exists until the insured person's death—assuming the premiums are paid. The three types of permanent policies are: whole life, universal, and endowment.

During divorce proceedings, the value of a permanent life insurance policy typically equates to the cash surrender value. If your husband has this type of policy, you would be best served to contact the insurance company directly to ascertain the current cash value and also to find out if there are any outstanding policy loans hubby may have "forgotten" to mention.

IT'S A FACT

Term life insurance may be a viable vehicle for the divorcing woman, depending upon the number of years she will receive alimony, among other considerations. If you will receive alimony for 10 years, you may well want to have a 10-year term insurance policy on your husband in case he dies before he pays you the alimony that ceases upon his death. Talk to your CDFA before deciding how to proceed.

Chapter 13

Home Matters

"La Casa Costa Lotta."

*— Sign outside a glamorous Tuscan-style
home in rural San Diego County*

DOES YOUR CASA—AKA HOUSE—COST A lot of money
to maintain?

Two months after paying off the house she bought
several years ago upon her divorce, a friend watched
$10,000 go down the sewer drain for emergency repairs.
In addition to discovering the answer to the age-old
question, "Do plumbers really have plumbers' cracks?"
(Yes.), she realized to her chagrin that she would have to
start saving all over again toward major projects such as
a new roof.

Fortunately, during her divorce proceedings, she had
made what at the time was an anguished decision. She
allowed her ex to keep their bucolic home studded with
fruit trees on a secluded acre and planted herself and her
teenage son in a less expensive, less expansive, but still
charming home.

Her ex ultimately let the house fall into foreclosure while she flourished, albeit on a less-extravagant scale than before. Over the years, thanks to prudent financial planning, she was able to amass the funds needed to cover the sewer repair while remaining financially afloat.

Everyone's situation is different. It is important to work with a knowledgeable financial professional who understands real estate tax issues and arcane home division rules, including "use period" and "ownership period," as they relate to divorce.

Your financial advisor—preferably a CDFA who is steeped in the esoteric intricacies of marital home issues—can: 1) calculate the cost basis and capital gain should you and your husband choose to sell your home; 2) research and present alternatives; and 3) help you understand the financial viability and liability of one party keeping the home.

IT'S A FACT

Since divorce is a major financial transaction, one significant and often contentious issue is who gets the house. For many, this conundrum resonates on an emotional as well as financial level. It is crucial not to let emotions reign over reality.

A divorcing couple needs to consider the equity (or lack of it) they have built in their home. If the house is "under water"—meaning they owe more on their mortgage than the house is currently worth—they are in a quandary. They cannot sell the home and divide the equity because there is no equity to divide.

Another option—one spouse buying out the other—may not work if neither spouse is able to maintain the home on their own. In negative equity cases such as this, a CDFA can actually help both parties find the least painful and most equitable solution.

IT'S A FACT

Continuing joint ownership of the home post-divorce until the kids are grown can seem like an attractive possibility. But the variables (e.g., property value fluctuations, interest rates) affecting the eventual sale can be stressful, not to mention the forced ongoing connection between exes.

Software Makes Hard Choices Easier

At age 53, Judy thought she had it all: a gorgeous, five-bedroom home on two acres in an exclusive California community; an eminently successful husband of twenty-nine years with a high, six-figure annual salary; and two academically gifted sons attending prestigious universities.

SIDEBAR

It all changed in an instant when Judy's husband coldly informed her that he had met someone new and intended to divorce her. Torn asunder from everything she'd taken for granted, Judy was determined to cling to the last vestige of her past happy life—her home.

As her CDFA, I used a sophisticated planning software program to create simulations, analyze investment returns and risks, present probable scenarios, and ultimately, offer a solution to secure her financial welfare—not just in the short term, but for the rest of her life.

I initiated a frank conversation. I told her I empathized deeply with her situation, but that we had to prioritize expenses to increase her chances of not running out of money in her lifetime.

It took some time and effort on my part, and some serious soul-searching on her part, but eventually, Judy realized she needed to downsize and make major life changes. She sold her home and bought a low-maintenance condo, using money from the sale to buttress her investment accounts. She reduced her discretionary spending and found a part-time job working for a nonprofit organization for which she had previously volunteered. She regained her tennis stroke and positive outlook on life. She indulged in a sparkling makeover, branched out to make new friends, and planned trips to visit her sons at college.

Most of all, she felt confident and secure in her new singlehood. If she met someone, great, she told me. But if not, like the independent star of *The Mary Tyler Moore Show*, she knew she could make it on her own.

Note to Reader: Judy is an amalgam of several clients I have helped over the years. Although a composite, Judy is emblematic of women who emerge on the other side of divorce with a strength and resiliency they did not realize they had.

Consider Making a Clean Break and a Fresh Start

There are numerous reasons you may want to keep your marital home and equally compelling reasons to split/sell, downsize, and move on with your life. If you make the latter decision, knowing you will be able to afford to buy and maintain your new home can empower and energize you.

Once you acknowledge the emotional attachment you have to your home, you can deal with the memories of your family history there: your bonds with neighbors and the neighborhood; your anxiety about relocating; and the sheer comfort of familiarity. After you examine these feelings, you will be much better able to research your options objectively and make the wisest choice. Then, whether you decide to or are forced to leave your home, you can remain in control of your destiny.

Just as you can take the antique oak sideboard and other cherished pieces to your new home, while disposing of the kitchen table you have come to dislike, you can take your many happy memories with you and dispose of the bitter moments. Your new home will have the absolutely most important element in it: you and your peace of mind.

A Final Note: You may want to consider installing a trampoline in your new backyard because, believe it or not, once you are on the other side of this ordeal, you may well feel like jumping for joy!

Chapter 14

The Dating Game

"It's not the men in my life that count; it's the life in my men."

— *Mae West*

REMEMBER BACK IN YOUR SALAD days when "social security" meant having a date on Saturday night? Now, here you are, suddenly single due to divorce or death with actual Social Security headed your way.

Even if getting a divorce was your idea, you may feel adrift. If you're an empty nester, you might feel very much alone, rambling around in a big house all by yourself. And now that you're not part of a couple, you perhaps are left out of dinners and other activities you previously attended with your ex.

So what's a mature single woman to do? My advice: Dive back into life. Just because one boat sank should not prevent you from diving gracefully back into the water. Just don't forget your life (and wallet) preserver!

Look at All Those Fish in the Sea

It helps to view your current situation not as a frightening challenge, but an exhilarating opportunity. Tell yourself, "The time to be happy is now and the place to be happy is right where I am."

You can find books, blogs, magazines, and websites devoted to dating later in life. Instead of duplicating their advice, I will share some nuggets of my own.

If you're looking for love online, no need to beware the Internet, but be wary. Sadly, there are wolves in sheep's clothing out there pretending to be someone they are not so they can fleece you.

As a teenager, your parents probably told you to guard against guys who were "out for only one thing." Well, that thing some guys may want from you now is your money. On the other hand, millions of people have met their match on dating sites, so feel free to give it a whirl.

Old-school ways of meeting men still apply. In fact, speaking of school, many folks have rekindled relationships with former classmates at their 30th and even 40th high school reunions. (OMG, that dorky kid in your freshman math class morphed into a hunky successful businessman!)

Make Your Move

Perhaps you and your husband drifted apart because you had so few interests in common. This is the perfect occasion for you to sample forgotten or fresh activities. Join a gym. Learn to play an instrument. Check out enrichment programs offered through your local community college or city recreation department. Affordable classes in everything from hula dancing to pottery making abound. You may or may not find a match made in heaven, but you will have a devil of a good time acquiring new talents and new friends.

You can also find love at your local humane society or pet rescue organization. Sure, your furry bestie might shed on your bed, but you'll experience unconditional love. Walking a dog is a great way to meet people and socialize with pet owners; it also gets you out of the house, away from your troubles, and on the move.

If you are having trouble moving forward and are unsure where to turn and what to do with this new chapter in your life, consider working with a dating and relationship coach such as my friend Traci Porterfield (see sidebar). Traci is a self-described "eternal optimist dedicated to helping you find the love of your life." The investment you make to ensure "what's next is better" can pay dividends for years to come.

The important thing is to take the first step. Even a bad date is part of the process, and it gives you something to laugh about later.

My ultimate advice: Be enthusiastic. There are adventures all around. If you look for them, you'll find them. They'll find you.

Choose Empowerment and Seek Love by Design

SIDEBAR

Traci Porterfield, the ebulliently positive and positively ebullient CEO/Founder of Love by Design, has worked with motivational gurus Tony Robbins and Deepak Chopra, so her approach to mature-age dating is holistically-centered.

She believes, "What you put in your head is what will happen. It is imperative that you view your past through the lens of how lessons learned will help you move forward. Instead of feeling rage against your ex, consider the good things that came from the relationship."

Traci acknowledges, "Finding yourself in this stage may be scary; it is unknown and uncomfortable. But just as you must accept the past, you should own the present so you can future-pace yourself into a better tomorrow."

On her website, *www.MyLovebyDesign.com*, Traci offers her book *10 Ways to Raise Your Dating IQ!* She also presents one-on-one coaching programs, online dating advice, and a questionnaire that identifies and addresses issues that may be holding you back.

Above all, Traci emphasizes, "Choose empowerment." I agree!

Chapter 15

Plan Be

"It is never too late to be what you might have been."

— George Eliot

S OME THINGS IN LIFE—THE LOSS of a job, the shattering of a precious heirloom—you will eventually get over. Others—the loss of a parent, the shattering of a years-long marriage—you may not be able to get over, but you must get through.

Whether you get over or get through the dramas and traumas, you need to summon the will to somehow get *beyond* them so you can become whole again and enjoy a happy, productive, and fulfilling life.

It's not easy.

Goodbye, Plan A

"On my forty-ninth birthday, I decided that all of life was hopeless and I would eat myself to death." That is the first sentence of *Plan B* by insightful and witty author Anne Lamott. We've all been there.

In 1969, psychiatrist Elisabeth Kübler-Ross posited the five stages of grief in terminal illness. The chronological stages apply to a number of life-changing contexts, including divorce.

Stage 1: Denial…No, this cannot be happening to me!

Stage 2: Anger…Why me? This is not fair!

Stage 3: Bargaining…Maybe if I have sex with him more often (and let him do "that thing"), we can save our marriage.

Stage 4: Depression…I am so sad. Nothing has any meaning for me anymore.

Stage 5: Acceptance…It's going to be okay. I am going to be okay.

Hello, Plan B

The end of your "happily ever after" can signal a new beginning, but you must let go of any bitterness and recognize that being rooted to an angry past will prevent you from growing toward a shiny future.

It sounds trite, but you: Must. Move. On. Having a financial advisor—in particular, a Certified Divorce Financial Analyst—as your partner can be essential to the divorce process and subsequent healing.

When confronted with an impending divorce, most people race to find an attorney. But if you wait to tackle the financial issues until later in the proceeding or, worst-case scenario, after the agreement has been finalized, it may be too late.

Pre-divorce financial counseling can give you the knowledge and confidence to take control of your finances and regain control of your life. A CDFA will help you research your options and avoid getting ensnared in rushed, unwise decisions urged upon you by your spouse.

An Ass with Assets

Sam and Sandra were getting a divorce. Sam wanted the divorce. Sandra did not and, in fact, was mired in stage three (bargaining) of grief. During their fifteen-year marriage, Sam made almost all of the financial decisions, including what to invest in and how much to invest.

SIDEBAR

Unsurprisingly, Sam, in his benevolent dictator role, patronizingly told Sandra, "We will simply split our assets 50/50. You take this half. I'll keep this half."

After years of allowing him to manage the money, Sandra acquiesced. The judge who granted the divorce saw nothing amiss with the asset division.

Only later did Sandra realize she'd been duped by her duplicitous ex. Due to the types of assets Sam had given her, and the types of assets he had kept, he could access his half tax-free while she would have to pay taxes on her half when she accessed them.

E.R. Docs Do Not Provide Holistic Care

Divorce attorneys are eminently qualified in their field. Many have the wisdom to understand that the intricacies of financial details, including tax issues and division of assets, are beyond their realm of expertise.

Your attorney has your best interests in mind but focuses on the immediate situation. Divorce attorneys are a bit like emergency room physicians: they want to get you through the crisis in one piece. Because they know their limitations and your needs, wise divorce attorneys frequently bring financial experts like me into the process at the beginning. Ideally, I am your first point of contact and can find and coordinate appropriate professional resources on your behalf.

My Approach: Professional, Personable, and Always on Your Side

As a conscientious, compassionate member of your divorce team, I work with you before divorce proceedings begin. I work with you and the team during the process. I am here for you after the divorce is finalized.

Typically, our first consultation is a warm and friendly conversation. I want to get to know you so I can best serve you. Establishing a rapport is vital if we are to be open and candid with one another.

Sometimes, a traumatic event such as divorce or death can trigger long-buried, painful memories from childhood or early adulthood—things that you forgot happened but now dominate your consciousness. In a case such as this, I may suggest you visit a therapist.

As we work through the divorce process, I will help you understand the financial issues and consequences of each decision. We will go into deep detail on everything you need to know before, during, and after your divorce: from analyzing retirement plans to assessing the advantages and disadvantages of keeping your marital home, developing a budget, and moving forward with optimism and joy. It's all part of the complete and comprehensive package I provide.

I cannot promise I will always tell you what you want to hear, but I promise I will always tell you what you need to know. And I will always have your back.

P.S. BTW, I have never thrown a frying pan at my husband.

Deana Carter

Bibliography

Brown, Susan L. and Lin, I-Fen. The Gray Divorce Revolution: Rising Divorce Among Middle-Aged and Older Adults, 1990-2010. Bowling Green, OH: Bowling Green State U, 2012.

Busch, William K. *The Money Ride*. La Jolla, CA: Kala Publishing, 2016.

Divorce Financial Analyst Journal, Institute for Divorce Financial Analysts, January-March 2019; April-June, 2019.

"Financial do's and don'ts of divorce." Fidelity Viewpoint, 2016.

Goldie, Daniel C. and Murray, Gordon S. *The Investment Answer*. New York, NY: Hatchett Book Group: 2011.

Green, Janice. Divorce After 50...Your Guide to the Unique Legal & Financial Challenges. NOLO, 2013.

Hiltzik, Michael. "Insurers slip up, seniors suffer." *Los Angeles Times*. July 28, 2019.

"How to protect finances if you're widowed or divorced." Fidelity Viewpoint, 2017.

"Medicare & You." *U.S. Government Medicare Handbook.* Baltimore, MD: 2019.

Morris, Kenneth M. and Siegel, Alan M. *The Wall Street Journal Guide to Personal Finance.* New York, NY: Lightbulb Press, 1997.

Morris, Kenneth M. and Virginia B. *The Wall Street Journal Guide to Understanding Money & Investing.* New York, NY: Lightbulb Press, 1999.

Porterfield, Traci. www.mylovebydesign.com. 2019.

"Retirement Benefits." Social Security Administration, 2017.

Steverman, Ben. "Middle-age divorce is especially brutal." *Los Angeles Times.* July 29, 2019.

"The Fundamentals of Divorce: Modules One, Two, Three, and Four." Institute for Divorce Financial Analysts. Durham, NC: CertiTrek Publishing, 2016.

"What Matters Most…A woman's guide to an inspired retirement strategy." Prudential, 2013.

Selected Online Resources

Deana Carter, CLU, ChFC, CDFA: www.carterfinancial.biz; deana.carter@LPL.com

Free Annual Experian, Equifax, and Transunion Credit Reports: www.annualcreditreport.com

Institute for Divorce Financial Analysts: https://institutedfa.com/

Medicare: www.medicare.gov

For local help with Medicare, Kelli Graham (858) 756-8889 kelli@kgrahaminsurance.com

National Domestic Violence Hotline: www.thehotline.org; 800-799-7233

National Foundation for Consumer Credit: www.nfcc.org

Social Security Administration: www.ssa.gov

For local help with, or Complimentary credit consultation go to www.b2cr.com

About the Author

DEANA **CARTER,** OF
CARTER FINANCIAL, is a
licensed financial advisor who
has developed an exemplary
reputation during her nearly
three decades of assisting
individuals and businesses
achieve their financial and
lifestyle goals. A specialist in
women's issues, she is fluent
in tax law and other topics
related to divorce and has the
ability to provided expert witness testimony in several
types of court cases.

Deana has set herself apart in a crowded, highly
competitive field by thinking boldly outside the box;
challenging conventional financial wisdom, when appropriate; customizing strategies to address each individual's
unique circumstances, aspirations, and needs; and mar-

shaling/coordinating professional resources to envelop the client in a cocoon of reassuring security.

A longtime Charter Life Underwriter (CLU) and Charter Financial Consultant (ChFC), Deana successfully completed a rigorous curriculum to attain Certified Divorce Financial Analyst (CDFA) status. One of only 5,000 CDFAs in the U.S., Deana undertook this challenge because she is passionate about helping women understand the economic issues facing them during divorce negotiations and optimizing their financial settlements, thus enabling them to live their best lives now and in the future.

Deana earned a Bachelor of Business Administration degree, with a minor in Economics. She studied Comparative Economics at the University of Oxford and holds an Associate of Science degree in Civil Engineering.

Deana is committed to serving her San Diego area community, with a focus on residents in need, particularly women and children. She founded and continues to chair Women Benefitting the Community and is an active member of other service organizations. She is very involved with Nice Guys, a part of San Diego since 1979, helping local families who have fallen on tough times. She serves as board treasurer and investment advisor of the Rancho Santa Fe Library Guild and as treasurer for the Rancho Santa Fe Golf Board. An avid outdoor adventurer, Deana has climbed Mt. Kilimanjaro, completed the Baja 500 on her motorcycle, and competed in a Dog Fight simulated combat in a 1979 Varga aircraft.

Deana Carter resides with her husband, John Ingalls, in Rancho Santa Fe, California. For more information, visit *www.CarterFinancial.biz* or *www.BootorBury.com*.

About Carter Financial

DO YOU …

- feel prepared to make wise financial decisions for your circumstances today … and in the future?
- have a plan to reach your retirement goals, protect your financial assets and generate income so you can live comfortably for the rest of your life?
- understand pensions, annuities, stocks, bonds, and other financial products? How about government programs such as Social Security and Medicare?
- feel confident that you can manage your financial resources to maintain your standard of living and quality of life?

Deana Carter Can Provide a Financial Framework

For a limited time, author Deana Carter, CLU, ChFC, CDFA, is offering readers of this book a complimentary, customized financial assessment so you can move forward confidently to manage your wealth and well-being now and for decades to come.

The founder of Carter Financial, Deana has amassed three decades of experience working with individuals and businesses to assess financial goals, provide clear explanations of financial products and services, and offer a personalized roadmap to achieve a confident financial future. As an LPL Financial Advisor, she is affiliated with one of the leading financial services companies and the largest independent broker/dealer in the nation.

To schedule your complimentary, customized, no-obligation financial assessment, contact Deana Carter at 858.756.1566 or deana.carter@lpl.com.

BOOK DEANA CARTER
TO SPEAK
AT YOUR NEXT EVENT

IF YOU ARE LOOKING FOR a financial expert who can make financial education fun, look to Deana Carter, CLU, ChFC, CDFA, as your next speaker. She also is available to sign copies of this book, *WHAT TO DO IF YOU BOOT HIM OR BURY HIM.*

Deana is an accomplished keynote speaker who is highly skilled at creating engaging presentations that connect immediately with audiences in an informative and entertaining way.

As one of only 5,000 Certified Divorce Financial Analysts in the United States, she is especially attuned to women's issues and is passionate about helping women successfully navigate challenging situations such as divorce or spousal death.

Deana's approach to financial matters is far from dry. Utilizing real-life examples presented in a witty manner, she possesses a unique ability to share serious information in a humorous way that she hopes will leave your event-goers LOL all the way to the bank.

To ascertain Deana Carter's availability as a speaker for your event, contact Deana at 858.756.1566 or deana.carter@lpl.com.